ANCHOR BOOKS

SEASON OF GOODWILL

Edited by

Heather Killingray

First published in Great Britain in 2004 by
ANCHOR BOOKS
Remus House,
Coltsfoot Drive,
Peterborough, PE2 9JX
Telephone (01733) 898102

All Rights Reserved

Copyright Contributors 2004

SB ISBN 1 84418 329 7

Foreword

Anchor Books is a small press, established in 1992, with the aim of promoting readable poetry to as wide an audience as possible.

We hope to establish an outlet for writers of poetry who may have struggled to see their work in print.

The poems presented here have been selected from many entries, and as always editing proved to be a difficult task.

I trust this selection will delight and please the authors and all those who enjoy reading poetry.

Heather Killingray
Editor

CONTENTS

The Rocking Chair	Ian W Robinson	1
Feisty Festive Felines	Leigh Crighton	2
Number Eleven 2002 AD	Carol Ann Darling	3
The Phenomenon At Christmas	Lachlan Taylor	4
Christmas Time	Ben Wilkinson	5
At Christmas Time	T Clarke	6
Make Her Day	Jon El Wright	7
Deliveries	G J Cayzer	8
A Christmas Verse	Albert E Bird	10
Christmas Is Snowless	M D Bedford	11
Santa's Busy Workshop	Christine M Tracey	12
Wishing You A Very Happy Christmas	S L Astley	14
Christmas Gladness	Wesley Stephens	15
Dear Santa	Mark Wndsor Oldfield	16
Christmas Time	Rosemary Platt	17
Christmas Is Over	Harold Clarke	18
Christmas (2)	David Xeno	19
Jingle all The Way: The Gift Of Christmas	Delroy Dwyer	20
Merry Christmas Santa Happy New Year!	Denis Martindale	21
A Christmas Wish	Pat Weaver	22
Home For Christmas	D M Neu	23
Another Calamity At Christmas	Carol Burton	24
Toyshop?	Anna Shannon	25
Jingle All The Way	Len Woodhead	26
Springtime	Mary Joan Boyd	28
On This Special Day	Somen Sen	29
Untitled	Sheila Redpath	30
Ho! Ho! Ho! It's Christmas	Ken Davidson	32
The Mustard Yellow Dress	Norma Rudge	33
A Teenage Christmas	Laura P Williams	34
A Christmas Card From Loulé	Audrey J Roberts	35
What Does It Mean To You?	Pamela Carder	36
Nativity	Helen M Seeley	37

Christmas Raining In Southern Snows	R Fekete	38
Christmas Dreams	Linda Knight	40
If We Would Only Know	Gerald S Bell	42
Has Santa Been Yet?	Jo Taylor	43
The Little Christmas Angel	C R Slater	44
A Family Christmas	Jennifer Collins	45
Christmas Cheer	Gill Smith	46
Winter's Warning	Janet Vessey	47
Friendly Christmas	Alexandra Osunwoke	48
Christmas Today	C S Snow	50
Christmas Fair	Alex Branthwaite	51
Christmas Present	Frank L Appleyard	52
Open Immediately - Gift Enclosed	David Varley	53
Two Hearts	M J Banasko	54
Twelfth Night	Alex Anderson	56
Discarded Tree	Henry Disney	57
Christmas Message	Margaret B Baguley	58
Christmas	D J Totten	59
Build Up	K Townsley	60
Christmas	Gwen Liddy	61
Christmas Corrected	Sarah Blackmore	62
On My Own . . .	Margaret Berry	63
Thank God For Christmas	Joan Earle Broad	64
Please - Don't Spoil Christmas	Sheila Bates	65
Winter's Operetta	John Clarke	66
Christmas	Gillian Ashe	67
Flannel On A Snowy Afternoon	Nick Zegarac	68
The Cheerful Postman	Clive Goldsmith	69
Chorus Line	Joyce Haigh	70
Christmas Wish	Gatekeeper	71
Christmas: Yuletide	Jonathan Pegg	72
Then And Now	Joan M E Gray	73
A Tale Of Two Christmas'	Gillian L Wise	74
Christmas Card Poem - 2003	Alan Dudeney	75
Christmas Stars On Ashdown Forest	Lorna Tippett	76

The Message	Rose Moss	78
A Snowflake Fell	David M Walford	79
Turkey	Ashley Smith	80
It's Christmas	Lynne Walden	81
Thoughts After Christmas	Jean Heath	82
Festive Folly From A Silly Wally	Paul Foreman	83
Christmas Eve	J H Scrafton	84
A Christmas Stocking	Marion Skelton	85
A Time To Remember	Keith C L Ball	86
The Tree	Anne Sackey	87
Christmas	P Brewer	88
Christ's Day - Or Ours?	Gillian Edge	89
A Sense Of Christmas	Claire Miller	90
A Fireside Story	H Cotterill	91
Christmas	Ann Wood	92
Christmas Star	Kathy Rawstron	93
Untitled	Mary Patton	94
Santa's Coming	Ladee Basset	95
Christmas - Enjoy Or Endure?	Bernadette Ince	96
Early December	Kathy Flanary Nelson	97
Tomato Sauce	P J Littlefield	98
The Alternative Christmas	Alison Jane Lambert	100
The Census In Bethlehem*	Norman Bissett	102
Christmas	Christine	104

THE ROCKING CHAIR

Rocking chair gently rocks,
glistening baubles hang around.
Fibre optics rival TV flicker,
untouched presents around the tree.
Silence of silent night.

Rocking chair gently rocks,
tinsel rustles in a breeze.
Smiling lips recall
children's laughter of long ago.
Silence of the first Noel

Rocking chair gently rocks,
new slippers scrape the rug.
Glass of amber nectar untried,
finger tips caress uncollected teddy bear.
Silent Christmas carols.

Rocking chair gently rocks,
white crystals to frozen tears
across the windowpane.
Flickering embers flicker no more.
Silent blue lips, forgotten festival of time.

Ian W Robinson

FEISTY FESTIVE FELINES

Oh tiresome dawn
you're here again
I've waited on you
since half-past ten
the eve before
with empty teacups,
last year's cards and unwrapped gifts
littered on the bedroom floor.

Strike up dawn chorus
your time is due
with melody so bright and sharp
as shone the moon the night before.
Bathing in steaming scented air
counting sheep, geese and even hair
a sleeping pill downed
with warming milk and usual care
loving tunes, selling songs
to a musical ear
but sleep was never counted there.

Soft sunshine now
with golden glare
lights on sleepy sleekit
coat of cats their
yellow eyes stare
accusingly as if to say
'Too late now to sleep -
night's gone - it's Christmas Day!'

Leigh Crighton

NUMBER ELEVEN 2002 AD

Thou shall not disrespect the Earth and waters
Of my beautiful creation with rubbish!
Listen to me for I am the Lord Thy God.
I am commanding a *sin!*
Litter blowing in the wind.
Put it all in the bin.
The empty drink tin.
Put them all in the bin.
Then take it all for recycling.
Along pathways and roadways,
Newspapers, sweet wrappers, plastic bags, empty cigarette packs
And butts galore.
What do you think a bin is for?
Put it all in.
To fail is a *sin!*
Dumped metal, mattresses and furniture etc in woods and country lanes,
It's a *sin!*
Take it for recycling.
Even in some rivers and seas,
Are thrown those supermarket trolleys.
Honour this land I created for you,
For I am angering!
Do not dump rubbish!
For it is now a *sin!*

Carol Ann Darling

THE PHENOMENON AT CHRISTMAS

Christmas is here, people's actions can tell
as they emerge from out of their shell
For months before they would never speak
and kept their tongues between their cheeks

This is a phenomenon most every year
as Christmas brings its days of cheer
Everyone wishes to be your friend
and cards to you they've already penned

Is it Christ's birthday which is the reason for this
that people you meet want to hug and kiss?
I would like to think so in this world of pain
where ugly crimes can leave such a stain

To love and befriend at Christmas time
must be admired within a Christian clime
When these few days friendships are gone and past
we must change our ways so they may last

Friendship can build a bridge of peace
where enmities among Nations forever cease
To nurture friends must be our quest
for without friendship, their is much unrest

Lachlan Taylor

CHRISTMAS TIME

C hildren open their presents
H appy as can be
R udolph's red nose is glowing
I cicles hanging from the tree
S anta brought all those cards and toys
T o the little girls and boys
M istletoe hanging on the wall
A lso, decorations in the hall
S now is building up, so tall!

T o you all, a Merry Christmas
I hope you enjoy yourselves
M ay love and peace be with you
E ven Santa's elves!

Ben Wilkinson (9)

AT CHRISTMAS TIME

It's Christmas time, it's Christmas time
sing hip hip hooray
join hands my friends and sing a song
in lands so far away,
remember why we celebrate
remember Christ the king,
so lift your voices loud and clear
and let the church bells ring.

The holly and the mistletoe
are hung for all to see,
the fairy smiles and waves her wand
from high up on our tree.
The town is white and frosty now,
old Santa's gone away,
a snowman smiles to greet the world,
down where the children play.

Old robin sings a merry tune,
and hops about the lawn,
he sits upon a Christmas card,
and comes to us each dawn,
we dance around the old spruce tree,
to celebrate a boy,
he came to Bethlehem last night,
to bring us peace and joy.

It's Christmas time, it's Christmas time,
sing hip hip hooray,
join hands my friends and sing a song,
on this new Christmas Day,
on this new Christmas Day!

T Clarke

MAKE HER DAY

Hip, hip, hip - hip hip - hoorah!
It's time for fun on Christmas Day
Show your friends your inner charms
Kick those legs and wave your arms
Relax and dance the hours away
Encourage the kids with toys to play
Your emotions do set free
Put your gifts below the Christmas tree
Spare a thought for He above
Embrace the one who you do love
Thank the barman over there
Seek to hide that love affair
Try to find the card you sent
Then fall asleep, deeply content
Dream of fun that you've just had
Shake the hand of old grandad
But throughout all, did you then think
About the one attached to the sink?
One who got things under way
The one who *made* this Christmas Day
Forgotten she has a broken heart
Now in tears as you depart
Now that all is over and done
Go through now to thank your mum
Without her grace, there'd be no brood
Why leave her now - misunderstood
You shared the feast that she prepared
Hug her now to show you cared -
It was she who made this great
Thank her now, tomorrow could be too late!

Jon El Wright

DELIVERIES

Twenty-five past to leaving time. Snowflakes are falling, always a positive sign . . . helps with the atmosphere. Snow without Christmas is as bad as Christmas without snow. You know what I mean? Pity the weather can't be right in all those hot places like Australia. Hard to imagine having a Christmas dinner on a beach.

Father Christmas walks across the now quiet and empty assembly room floor. He takes one last look round.
'Nothing forgotten . . . excellent!' he roars. With the magic sack over his shoulder, he checks himself in the mirror attached to the assembly room door. This mirror is magic. Like the one in the fairytale.

'Boss you look great! Have a good journey.'
'Thank you Marlo . . . see you later!'
Mrs C is waiting outside. She is the real brains of the organisation but don't tell anyone I told you so.

'Come on now Father, it wouldn't do for you to be late.'
'Mother! how could I run this place without you?'
'Hush old man - you're making me blush. Be off with you. I don't want to rush. On your return I will tell you of the time when your father was late.'
'My father! Well I never knew . . .'

Things move on, times change, but the children, they remain the same. Lying in their beds, feigning sleep, looking through half-closed eyes, biding their time. 'Hey, was that . . . or was that just a shadow passing the bedroom door?'

Central heating! When that came to be commonplace. Away with the open fires and chimney breasts. All helps to make making deliveries a bit of a chore. '*Ha, ha!* no not really! Only pulling your leg. However there is always the drains . . .'

'Old man, what are you talking about - drains. Christmas gifts! Who knows what *stuff* has passed through there and if you think I am going to wash your uniform after . . .'

'Enough Mother, I must be on my way. Goodnight my love, until tomorrow.'

'Goodnight old man, take care and I hope you've got me something nice this year. No more oven gloves!'

'I will, I mean I won't - Oh wait and see woman! Merry Christmas.'

G J Cayzer

A Christmas Verse

Give me the Christmas of long ago,
When we'd peep through the windows, hoping for snow.
And the fire would roar up the chimney breast,
And Mother's cooking, was at its very best.

The table would groan with pickles and ham,
Christmas cake and tarts with raspberry jam.
Uncle Jim would come with Aunty Mabel,
And Father would sit at the head of the table.

We would have sliced peaches and fresh cream too,
And serviettes, both pink and blue.
We would pull the crackers, put on paper hats,
The noise would disturb our sleeping cats.

On the Christmas tree the lighted candles would shine,
Mother would carefully sip her Sherry wine.
Aunty Mabel would sing and I'd have to play,
You had to sing carols on Christmas Day.

Then after the tea, we children would play,
With the toys we'd received on Christmas Day.
These are the happiest memories that I find,
All deeply locked away, safe in my mind.

Albert E Bird

CHRISTMAS IS SNOWLESS

Christmas is not Christmas
In days of old, we'd snow
No more snowman making
Or balls made for to throw
Although they've snow in some parts
Melts and becomes ice
Oxygen's is away taken
So coldness not that nice

M D Bedford

SANTA'S BUSY WORKSHOP

Santa Claus is busy with all his little elves,
stacks and stacks of presents, placed neatly
on the shelves.
All the little reindeer who help pull
Santa's sleigh,
Are making sure they're strong enough
by eating lots of hay.

The fairy dancing round and round, is
always prettily dressed,
She sits on top of the Christmas tree - she
knows she is the best.
Stars are being polished so that they will
shine so bright,
Twinkling in the winter sky - like diamonds
in the night.

Chimneys being swept to make quite sure
they're clean,
For a sooty Santa should simply not be seen,
Snowy beard and smart red suit -
now a bigger size!
Santa's tum has grown lots more cos
he's eating too many mince pies.

The elves load up Santa's sleigh, while
the reindeer stand and wait,
Till his bright red face - with snowy beard
greets them at the gate.
Then he whispered in their ears some magic -
to make them fly,
With a jingle of their bells, they flew up to the sky.

So boys and girls be ready - hang your stockings
on the bed,
And make sure you all remember that Santa
must be fed.
He's up there in the sky right now,
flying very high,
But when he comes back down to earth,
he'll look for his mince pie.

When Santa has finished delivering presents
to all the girls and boys,
The reindeer will take him back again,
to the factory to make more toys.
So up where the stars are twinkling,
from the sleigh he takes one last peep,
At the snowy covered rooftops where the
children are still asleep.

The bells on the reindeer jingle a
very happy tune,
Santa's almost snoring as they fly right past the moon.
Another happy Christmas he hopes he has achieved.
For the boys and girls, when they open the presents
they have now received.

The reindeer land so gently by a cabin made of wood,
As Santa from the sleigh gets out -
at first he thought he could
Find a little room for one mince pie, but then
he shook his head,
I think I'm putting weight on - so I'll go to bed instead.

Goodnight - Merry Christmas!

Christine M Tracey

WISHING YOU A VERY HAPPY CHRISTMAS

W inter time is here again,
I ce and snow across the Glen,
S moking chimneys, chestnuts roasting
H ouses full of lots of toasting,
I n front of open fires
N o cross words or even wires!
G od made this a special time,

Y uletide, this word is fine.
O vens burning with turkeys full
U ncracked crackers, ready to pull.

A mazement on a child's face,

V ictorious, with no haste,
E njoying all the unwrapping
R easons not to be yapping.
Y es, we're onto the presents

H ustle and bustle, it's oh so pleasant,
A ghast at the thought of a doll
P erhaps it's time for a stroll.
P lenty of turkey now been ate,
Y es, you've guessed it, an empty plate.

C hristmas comes but once a year
H armonious, without any fear,
R ich puddings and mince pies
I f only my tummy ruled my eyes,
S tuffed full of all this food
T ime now for sleepy mood.
M ovies and games are after this,
A gain this Christmas, it's been just bliss
S anta to come again next year? We'll see!

S L Astley

CHRISTMAS GLADNESS

Christmas time has come again
Peace on Earth, goodwill to men
See the Yule log on the fire
Hear the merry festive choir
Sweet the message that they bring
Glory to the newborn king.

Now the gladness has begun
Let the steeple bells be rung
Wonder at the gracious plan
When our Lord became a man
Ponder at the angels strain
Peace on Earth, goodwill to men.

Jesus in our world did dwell
Jesus our Emmanuel
Peace the message that he brings
From the human heart it springs
Listen to the glad refrain
Peace on Earth, goodwill to men.

Wesley Stephens

DEAR SANTA

Dear Santa,
my dad's
lost his job
they've sent
it abroad.

My mum,
she left us,
six months ago.

If you don't
come to our
house, I'll
understand why!

Some Indian kids'
father, will now
have a job, and
some cash to keep
them fed by -

PS: Just send
my mum back.

Mark Windsor Oldfield

CHRISTMAS TIME

Time of laughter, merriment,
Time of friendliness and fun;
Giving and receiving;
Reunited family.
Time of cosiness and cheer,
Time of greetings and goodwill;
Unashamed indulgence
And a massive spending spree.

Time of tears and aching hearts,
Time of loneliness and loss;
Wistfully recalling
Christmases that used to be.
Time of pain and dark despair,
Time of hunger, homelessness;
Eking out a living,
Knowing only poverty.

Time of praise and thankfulness,
Time of worship, wonderment;
Kneeling in a stable
Where the Son of God is born.
Time of love and joy and peace,
Time of healing, hopefulness;
Welcome, Holy Child. Your
Coming, heralds God's new dawn.

Rosemary Platt

CHRISTMAS IS OVER

Christmas has gone - it went too quickly.
With so much food, we felt a bit sickly.
There were plenty of presents, you'd never believe,
And some arrived late on Christmas Eve.

Some leather gloves and a warm, woolly scarf.
A thick book of jokes to make me laugh,
And to keep us happy on wet afternoons,
Some music tapes with popular tunes.

And down at the church on Christmas Night,
We joined in the carols by candlelight,
And journeying home along the way
Saw houses lit up with festive display.

Cousins from London sent loud, snazzy ties,
And a brown leather belt which was quite the wrong size!
Auntie sent me those vivid check socks,
And fruit and nut chocolates in a bumper box.
A jar full of sweets and a PlayStation game
And granny's new photo in a smart, silver frame.

Fingering gift tags and handling with care,
Tugging bows and ribbons, wondering what was there.
Knee deep in paper from all this unwrapping,
But talcum powder gifts, were certainly lacking.

We had so much to eat, each holiday day
Our diet sheets were thrown away.
But after four days, our nerves were on edge
With endless cold turkey and surplus cold veg.

So Christmas is over and now once again,
Our bank accounts are feeling the strain.
Decorations and trimmings will soon disappear,
Hidden up in the loft until next year.

Harold Clarke

CHRISTMAS (2)

Where does Christmas come from? That's what I want to know!
Was it always so? This mish-mash of tales and traditions
mixed up with religions and commerce and creed and greed.
Was it ever wholesome?

Before Christ (or not - if you prefer) came day and night
easy to tell - one dark, one bright. Depending where you live,
the year would also have its time, its clime
of cold and hot.

In ancient winter, there were few plants to tend
few had lights to fend off darkness
there was so little could be achieved, they grieved
until the year got gentler.

So ancient man and woman are feeling gloomy,
their bellies feeling roomy, waiting for the days to lengthen
sun to strengthen, the year's day to say
spring is coming.

If you had it, why not burn fires for warmth and light
and with that sight, if food could be had,
feast and be glad that soon the gloom
would turn and take flight.

Mankind's self centred. We see others in terms of ourselves
the unseen are elves or angels, spirits, tame or wild
the year is born a child. Crossing the new threshold,
once old, we delight in the newness entered.

So we've got our cause for joy. It's redundant now,
farmers plant twice a year; a chemical boosting
gets seeds unseasonably thrusting, the same with beasts.
For feasts, we no more need a baby boy.

David Xeno

JINGLE ALL THE WAY: THE GIFT OF CHRISTMAS

Trees are put up, decorations displayed
Lights are put on, carols are played
Cards and gifts, if lucky . . . there's snow and ice-rain
Guess what is here? Yes, Christmas again!

The story of Christmas reminds us of peace and goodwill
Amidst the violence and the cold December chill
The world at large shares in the story it tells
'God with us' . . . E-mman-u-el!

The gift of Christmas is for one and all
The rich, the poor; old, young; great and small
Its messages ring out, very strong, loud and clear
With sounds of laughter and singing of good cheer.

The season's merry-making is for all to see
Public celebrations of this grand festivity
Pubs are full, functions well packed
Homes are crowded; fridge's well stacked . . .

. . . Of turkey and puddings, Christmas cakes and sweets
Drinks as well, to make up the treat
There are special programmes and favourite films to watch on TV
Events to look out for all the family.

And that's not all, there's still lots yet more
The less fortunate in the byways we cannot ignore
The homeless, the lonely, weary tramps and drunks in need
Hot soups are prepared and a bunk for to sleep.

There's a lot more to add, but time does not wait
Like Christmas it passes, you're either ready or late
So, the next time streets light up and snow falls from the air
Look out! The gift of Christmas once again is here!

Delroy Dwyer

MERRY CHRISTMAS SANTA HAPPY NEW YEAR!

Joys can come in many ways -
Especially on our Christmas Days:
New presents wrapped exquisitely . . .
New presents unwrapped expertly!
In times like these, the heart beats fast
For Christmas Day has come at last!
Excitement tempts us take a peak!
Remembered lists of gifts we seek!
If only all our days were so:
Season's wishes would overflow!
Look here! Look there! Look everywhere!
Our hopes and dreams fulfilled by prayer!
Visits by friends and folks we love -
Each acting gentle as a dove!
Lights on Christmas trees that cheer!
Yet Christmas joys come *once* a year!

Denis Martindale

A Christmas Wish

I have one wish for Christmas
if you could grant for me
an end to aching loneliness.
Someone to share with me.
A Christmas to remember
just one to call my own
and pull me from this black despair
the worst I've ever known.
I need someone to hold me
to know that I'm alive.
Someone to melt this block of ice
that's building up inside.
The happy festive season
is slowly drawing near.
Christmas, a season of goodwill -
but not for me this year.

Pat Wheaver

HOME FOR CHRISTMAS

Coming home in the dark
With the wind blowing,
We said to each other,
'Hurry - it will soon be snowing.'

I wanted to wait and see the snow,
Feel it soft on my face,
Watch it cover hedge
And field and secret place,
But we went on, until
At the crest of the hill,
We looked back at the town,
Now wearing lights in the darkness
Like a crown.

We went further and the snow came,
We slipped, bending over against the storm,
Struggling as the wind rose,
We longed for home where it was warm.

And then the bells began,
Peal after peal they rang,
Until the sound swirled with the snow
And our hearts sang.

For it was nearly Christmas,
And tomorrow we would go
And gather holly, the berries sharp
Against the snow.

We would bring in and decorate the tree,
Then wait through the night,
Longing for the morning
And the wonders to come with the light.

D M Neu

ANOTHER CALAMITY AT CHRISTMAS

I am so sorry, Emily!
Your lovely bowl is shattered.
For fifty years I cherished it
Because, to me, it mattered.

I'd written your obituary
When I was young and shiny-eyed.
I can't believe I'm older now
Than you were when you died.

You'd been a valued family friend;
The midwife at my hard-won birth.
Your nephew gave your bowl to me
In memory of your worth.

I used it; washed it; cared for it;
Remembering you each day.
It sat upon our table top
And held the fruit display.

It now joins Esther's tea pot;
Small fragments in the dust;
And once again I've wept vain tears
Because I broke a trust.

Carol Burton

TOYSHOP?

'So,' I said to the woman behind the counter,
'have you got a bow and arrow?'
I could tell this question had caused a sort of stir,
the look was vague, the eyes confused and narrow.
'No,' I explained.
'It's not a video or a DVD.
No, it's nothing to do with electricity.'
'A bow . . . and . . . arrow?' she repeats slowly.
'Have we got a bow and arrow?' she calls
(to the girl with roots and strange fancy fingernails).
'What does it look like?' replies the girl,
her eyes half-heartedly searching the shelves.
'No, it's not a make of personal CD player,
it's not a *CD Rom* or anything to do with electricity.'
She waits, staring blankly for my description.
'It's . . . a bow and *arrow!*
A simple device of wood and string
and arrows that sing with joy
before suckering monsters and terrifying
The spoilt boy next door.'
'Mmm, I haven't seen one of those,'
she sympathetically explains, whilst taking two steps back
and holding open the shop door.
'You could try Robinsons, they cater for the most unusual
or perhaps they just don't make
those contraptions anymore.'
'No, it's not a contraption,' I try to explain
and stepping from the store I say again,
'it's simple, just a simple, proper old-fashioned toy
for an ordinary boy!'

Anna Shannon

JINGLE ALL THE WAY

In a small stable many years gone by
Something strange was happening, there was a glare across the sky
Everyone that saw this was wondering why was there such a light
The shepherds out in the fields had never seen such a sight

Three wise men on their camel train who were moving through
                                                                  the night
Were watching in amazement, they had never seen a star so bright
So they headed straight for Bethlehem along the beam of light
Everyone was out by the roadside, it was causing quite a fright

But gradually as they got closer they saw a small stable by an Inn
And just tied up by the stable were two asses, but listen what's that din?
The three wise men they dismounted when they got to the stable door
And just inside the stable was Joseph, in the corner, on the floor

But the shepherds they were only interested in the noise that came
                                                                    from within
So they gently walked into the stable to see what was making that din
And when they saw a little baby they could not believe their eyes
Right above the manger with a hole above, the light shone in from
                                                                     the skies

Little did those wise men know that the history they could see -
That little baby Jesus sat upon his mother's knee
They said, 'Mary what are you doing in this stable so old?'
She said the Inn was full and outside, it was so cold

The wise men gave comforts and gifts for the newborn baby boy
And then they went outside, so surprised they felt, so mild and full
                                                                     of joy
They made their way across the deserts, their minds were wondering
What had they seen?
Little did those men know how important their journey had been!

As they made their way across the sand on that cold and bitter night
The strangers that they met had seen the star, shining bright
But they didn't know at that time what an important child had made
                                                                                     that din

News travelled very slowly in their world that they were in

When eventually the word was spread and that small child began
                                                                                              his task

The wise old men of Bethlehem thought - *if only we had asked!*

Len Woodhead

SPRINGTIME

Early May, the birds sing sweetly, spring is here at last,
But 'Hark the Herald Angels sing,' they're going at full blast,
Down the Garden Centre, the Christmas cards are out,
Christmas, Merry Christmas, what *is* it all about?

Surely we can put it off, while summer days are long?
Jingle Bells, Jingle Bells, let's not hear that song.
Instead think very deeply of Baby Jesus Christ,
To celebrate His birth in May, now that's not very nice.

Look upon your calendar towards the end of year,
December, twenty-fifth, His birthday now is here.
But blazing hot is sunshine, on this the longest day,
Look there on the beach, where children happy play.

Here in early August, no summer sales I see,
But signs declaring, 'Rush out now and buy your Christmas tree,'
Rush out now and fill the tills, bash your bits of plastic,
This festive season, once so short, is now just like elastic.

Where has all tradition gone, the orange in the stocking?
Greed and all commercial gain, it really is quite shocking.
Overdraft and overspent, living on our credit.
Buying stuff that we don't need, really, where's the merit?

Housing Benefit, Income Support, living on the State,
For many families in this land, not much on Christmas plates.
Cold homes, no fires, electric keys run out,
There's poverty in this fine land, of that there is no doubt.

Little Baby Jesus, born in a stable so bare,
Twinkling lights and tinsel. He really didn't care.
Forget the cards in early June, that's not what it's about,
But 'Peace on Earth. Goodwill to all.'
Is what we all should shout.

Mary Joan Boyd

ON THIS SPECIAL DAY

From the old chimney comes a stranger
With a sack full of gifts on his shoulder
Both cheeks and nose are red in colour
Travelled from afar with his reindeers.

The happy sounds of the children they can hear
Little footsteps run down the stairs.
Father, mother and grandad on his rocking chair.
Resplendent Christmas tree vividly stands there.

Fairy lights sparkle on the baubles, multicolour.
What is under the Christmas tree? They all wonder.
With mistletoe and wine, they dance and cheer
Then they sit down for the special turkey dinner.

Twenty-fifth of December is a family day affair.
Rejoice the resurrection, enjoy the grandeur.
Son of God has come with goodwill and prayer.
To reawaken the faith in all things good and fair.

This day of all days, remember to be charitable, to care
Our sick, elderly and the weak and spare
Some thoughts for the world-wide pain and hunger,
To end all bitterness and the violence of war.

He wishes peace, love and prosperity everywhere
There is nothing and no reasons for despair.
Rich man, poor man, all who can hear.
Auld Lang Syne, all ye, be of good cheer.

Somen Sen

UNTITLED

Christmas merry
Christmas joy
Love came down - a baby boy!

Christmas Spirit
Yuletide fun
Holy gift - precious one!

Season's greetings
'Winterfest'
Give me back my festive jest!

Bring on Santa
Toys galore
Children wanting - always *more!*

Mamon's Season
Winter's chill
Waiting for the Visa bill!

Christmas stuffing
Booze and beer
Over full of Christmas cheer!

Cold and homeless
Lost and weak
Needing food and warmth this week!

God is love -
Not Harrod's sale!
Give *them* help - *not* 'Save the Whale!'

Keep in mind -
The Credo's clear
Christ came down and God is here!

Give to others
Love the poor
Merry Christmas - open door!

Sheila Redpath

Ho! Ho! Ho! It's Christmas

Ho! Ho! Ho! it's here again, that *happy* Christmastime,
the time for Santa and jingle bells . . . and Jesus, down the line.

Ho! Ho! Ho! it's 'round once more, the festive season of fun,
a season of larders fit to burst and turkeys on the run!

Ho! Ho! Ho! we sup the wine and liquor flows like water,
there's drunken drivers on the roads, but it's Christmas . . .
Does it matter?

Ho! Ho! Ho! the trees are lit, there's singing everywhere,
it makes the lonely lonelier. But have fun . . . who really cares?

Ho! Ho! Ho! there's headache pills and stomachs all askew,
from gorgin' and boozin' greedily . . . then sickness down the loo!

Ho! Ho! Ho! the sales are on. We're queuin' at the doors,
with overdrawn credit cards stampedin' through the stores.

But ho! ho! ho! the magic bit that makes the hell worthwhile,
is to watch the little children with their big, excited smiles.

For they feel they're in a wonderland, where reindeer come to call,
So ho, ho, ho! enjoy yourselves . . . Merry Christmas one and all.

Ken Davidson

THE MUSTARD YELLOW DRESS

Oh dear, it's Christmas time again,
And that can only mean one thing,
I'll keep my nerve and stay quite sane,
I know for sure that phone will ring!
'I've made a dress,' my nan will say,
'It's ready for a fitting soon,
Please make it later on today
And if you can, call after noon!'
I set off up the hill at noon,
The dreaded fitting to endure,
I reach Rose Cottage all too soon
I hope the dress has some allure!
The fitting on the table top,
I turn round slowly while the pins,
Hold hem in place and make me hop,
The length is halfway down my shins!
I wanted lace, I wanted tuile -
Please give this dress to Aunty Lou.
In mustard, I'll just look a fool.
My cousins would like it, Sally or Sue!
I would love a dress in pink or white,
I don't mind polka dots or stripes,
With a sash that's silky and shiny bright.
Mustard yellow, gives me the gripes!
I am ungrateful, yes I know,
I'll go back home to baby Tess,
I'm sorry, the answer is a definite no,
I can't wear that mustard, yellow dress!

Norma Rudge

A Teenage Christmas

I thought I was too old for Santa Claus,
But still listened for sleigh bells in the night.
I thought I was too old to say I couldn't sleep,
But I still went to Midnight Mass to pass the hours.
I thought I was too old to hang up my stocking,
But I still put it on my bed, just in case.
I thought I was too old to avoid the cooking,
But I helped just a bit and drank the sherry.
I thought I was too old to play with children's toys.,
But I joined my brother on the floor.
I thought I was too old to believe in the Christmas story.
I just thought I was, but I wasn't really.
No one is too old to believe in Christmas.

Laura P Williams

A CHRISTMAS CARD FROM LOULÉ

Heralding the festive season, pale petals,
The first Almond Blossom, open on bare trees.
As chill, wintry winds swirl!

Excited children rush to peep in toy-filled shops.
Christmas lights sparkle against darkening skies
Strung, like stars, across cold streets.

At bustling street corners, from smoking charcoal burners,
Hot smells of roasting chestnuts drift slowly
As gypsy girls fill newspaper cones.

Decorated Christmas trees glitter in tiny front gardens
While, on neat Council lawns, white nativity scenes
Remind us what Christmas is about.

Audrey J Roberts

WHAT DOES IT MEAN TO YOU?

Christmas, what does it mean to you?
The birth of Jesus - in a manger bare
Or hot mince pies, mulled wine and festive fare?

Simple shepherds, guarding their flocks
On the hillside, night so cold and black.
Or 'Another parcel for me,' from Santa's sack?

The star, shining and twinkling in the East,
No room at the inn, bad news for two, so tired.
Or 'Less tonic, more gin! Are the fairy lights wired?'

A cold stable housed Mary, Joseph her spouse
A babe in a manger, a wee Holy child,
Or 'I'm off to the gym, then my hair restyled!'

Astride camels from far-off desert lands
Came three kings with gifts so fine.
'Five golden rings? Hot spiced wine?'

Mourn the innocents, victims of Herod's slaughter
Male children, all cruelly killed.
Or 'I hope my stocking is bulging, well filled.'

Double standards are these, midst all festive fuss,
Remember that first Christmas in Bethlehem
How, one night changed the world and all things, for all men.

Pamela Carder

NATIVITY

Shepherds praised
And heavenward gazed
As angels proclaimed Jesus' birth.

Wise men from afar
Followed the Star
That led to the King of Heaven and Earth

Cattle were lowing
As if knowing
This babe was the Messiah, the word.

All gathered there
In the stable bare
Drawn to worship their Saviour and Lord.

Helen M Seeley

CHRISTMAS RAINING IN SOUTHERN SNOWS

down Tolpuddle Avenue walk
dusky Queen's Market
sneezed in the murky drizzle

raucous Asian peasant voices screech
a young man urinates under a single star
onto the circular prism of bone containers

as southern snow rains by wavy corrugated iron prisms
drains and roads swim in the reincarnation
where once the Palace vegetables grew

crumbly sacks of rubbish lean against the road safety fences
as shoppers slide on human droppings, dropped from brown paper bags
stamped into concrete smudged paths

a single lit window in all our township
displays palms and snow-covered Christmas trees in harmony together
neon lights scream kebabish welcomes to our little townlet

monkey gods in plastic shoppers leaving Tescos
where Mrs Idi Amin's cafe reeks just around the corner
and over the bridge by the Underground to little Uganda

where the variable cultures reign supreme branded in shop windows
in our little Asian town
problem area labels with new old family values

Council's frown along with the indigenous
filled with alternative life-styles whole global lines
all the races and lives getting a leg up
our township miraculously accepts all . . .

round the corner, the ex Labour whip
with a mind of his own
wears out his life being penalised
in his age of late, out of his state pension

no one turns a hair here
twixt the convent and the mosque
some go up, some go down
protesting against actions squeezed

gently passes life even at Christmas idem
along with the Colonials
reclaiming Queen Victoria's promise

cultures meet
the strongest dominates
and everyone enjoys Christmas tide

after all the twenty-sixth
is the founder of Pakistan's birthday
so no betrayals as we all sing round the tree

R Fekete

CHRISTMAS DREAMS

The baby cried at four o'clock.
It woke the dog, who went amok!
I let him out into the snow,
An icy wind began to blow.
I looked up to a dark, clear sky
And saw a large star, twinkling high.
I thought I saw a sleigh above,
But then our dog gave me a shove.
I went inside to make a drink
And then the kids kicked up a stink.
'We've got no toys, it isn't fair,
Santa's forgot he doesn't care!'
I said, 'Go back to bed and sleep,
It's far too early and don't peep!'
They argued going back to bed,
But then, oh silence, overhead.
I fed the dog then heard a sound,
And thought Santa is on his round.
I peered into the lounge to see
Santa kneeling by the tree,
Placing all the presents there.
I dropped my cup and thought, *Oh dear!*
Santa looked at me and said,
'Happy Christmas, sleepy head!'
I recognised that face and thought,
'So that's the suit he must have bought!'
He kissed me then and said, 'I must go.
I've left the sleigh out in the snow.
I'll just put the reindeer away,
Then we can start our Christmas Day.'

I thought I heard bells ringing round,
No, it was the alarm clocks sound.
I went downstairs and made some tea,
The kids were playing happily.
I let the dog out in the snow,
An icy wind began to blow.
I looked into a dark, clear sky,
And saw a large star twinkling high . . .

Linda Knight

IF WE WOULD ONLY KNOW

A baby boy born for us long years ago
Within a stable - laid in manger, low.
Where sheep and oxen warmly greet the child.
Beyond - the darkness, chaos reconciled.

New light and love abound. Hear angels sing
'Peace on Earth' and joyful tidings bring;
The Word, the wisdom, wreathed in awesome glory!
Astounded shepherds, wise men told their story.

Darkness denied, disbanded disbelief;
Away with sorrow, sadness, banish grief.
A new beginning, set aside all strife;
Goodwill to all - renewed, a gift of life.

Remember still the scene, yet centuries old.
The Word made flesh, the promised one foretold,
Still dwells within if we would only know
The baby, born for us long years ago.

Gerald S Bell

HAS SANTA BEEN YET?

'Has Santa been yet?' I quietly said
'No! It's far too early, go back to bed
It's only midnight,' whispered Mum.
'Go back to your room and don't be glum.'
I went to sleep for a long time,
Got up to find out what would be mine.
'Has he come yet Mum?' I excitedly cried
'No! It's just past one and I'm really tired,
Go back to bed till it's time to rise
And then you might find a huge surprise.'
I trudged back as I was told I should
Disappointed and restless, it was no good.
I waited for what seemed like a week
My new presents I should now seek
'I'm getting up now, it must be late
I guess it's round half-past seven or eight.'
'No!' grumbled Mum. 'It's only three.
Go back to bed, just wait and see.'
Off I went to bed once more
This wasn't easy, it was a chore.
Santa must have been by now, I think
I couldn't sleep another wink.
I think, *I'll try counting sheep!*
I'm told it may help me go to sleep.
Just five minutes later I awoke
My mum was there, it was no joke
'Get up now, you sleepyhead.
Are you staying all day in bed?
Santa's been and gone, it's fine.
Get up now, it's half-past nine!'

Jo Taylor

THE LITTLE CHRISTMAS ANGEL

Taking his magical
Angel feather quill pen,
The angel writes once more
To do notes yet again.
This time he writes
With a smile on his face,
Remembering to make sad homes
A much happier place.
He thinks Christmas Day
That children world-wide
Should see a little magic
With eyes opened wide.
So he writes to do notes
With a magical twinkle,
That Christmas magic in children
He must surely sprinkle.
He recalls what it's like
Being a small child
And thoughts of Santa
With his eyes opened wide.
He remembers indeed the meaning
The truth of Christmas Day
And thinks in his magic sparkles
This also he shall relay.

C R Slater

A FAMILY CHRISTMAS

Bells a jingle, carols are sung
Children are peeping
Father Christmas may come!
Presents are wrapped, placed under the tree,
Biscuits and sweets, cakes and chocolates,
Come and see!

People come in and say hello,
Bringing cards and best wishes,
Have a drink, before they go.
The family is here,
The turkey is cooked,
We all sit down, hold a cheerful look!

The meal is wonderful,
The parcels unwrapped,
The look of amazement
As the crackers go *snap!*

Jennifer Collins

CHRISTMAS CHEER

A Merry Christmas
seems by far the best way,
when families gather;
when there's so much to do.
Stress levels rise;
tempers wear thin.

So let's raise a toast
to a Merry Christmas,
and promptly ensure it
by draining the glass.

Gill Smith

WINTER'S WARNING

It's growing cold now
And the nights are coming home
The sun in all its glory
Refuses to share its heat
And the fields have withdrawn
Their colours they are in retreat
Icy breath freezes your every word
Spoken and heard
And falls upon your ears in silence
The leaves once elevated
And out of reach
Now lie carpeted at our feet
And the wind that cooled us
In summer's heat
Now warns us of rain, snow and sleet
Imprisoned, we must be
Or face that that decidedly will be
Frost on the other hand
Gives no warning
But appears instantly at dawning
Majestic in its ermine stole
Treachery is its main goal
And snowflakes fall
Like blossoms in the spring
But this blossom has winter's sting
And brings the robins out to sing
Who tell us don't be glum.
Spring will come, spring will come

Janet Vessey

FRIENDLY CHRISTMAS

Christmas season is a friendly season,
a festivity, a time to reconcile.

Grown men are like children,
children are like excited chickens.

No one can do wrong
but God help anyone
who makes excessive noise.

We hate other people
who jump, dance and laugh
too much and
while two thirds of adults
would celebrate the festivity,

nearly half of us would
have it banned.

Incessant loud music and laughter
drives us to the drink of
violence.

Yet subjecting them to untold torture
in the chamber of your imagination
usually has to suffice.

Christmas is golden
a time for silent reflections
on the year past.

A time for conscious thought
for the less fortunate.

If I could buy a house of gold
that would be nothing compared to what I owe you
for the gift you gave so graciously.

You wore a crown of thorns,
nails in your hands and your feet.

All this without a word
that's the kind of love
I near heard.

Alexandra Osunwoke

CHRISTMAS TODAY

The weeping bells
and Stockbroke Wells
tinkering our heart strings
like a fake
old classic.

C S Snow

CHRISTMAS FAIR

The opulent food fever is in full swing
As westerners dine in splendour
Stuffing bloated bodies with festive foodstuffs.
'I wish I had two bellies to fill.'

Christmas feeding frenzy is high
Higher than butter mountains
That are multiplying faster than credit card bills.
'I wish I had two bellies to fill.'

An African dawn welcomes a parched day
That shrivels staple maize crop again,
Hunger pervades and children cry.
'I wish my belly was half full.'

People are pawns in a permanent war
And bedraggled life is so cheap
As corrupt politicians flounder in search of peace.
'I wish my belly was half full.'

Alex Branthwaite

CHRISTMAS PRESENT

'Ring out the bells! It's Christmas Day!'
'Be jubilant!' the angels say.
All glory to our God and King
With chorused-anthems let us sing.

A newborn baby, weak and small,
Means great redemption for us all.
Today we shall, with heart and voice,
The gospel sound: 'Rejoice! Rejoice!'

With gifts and presents celebrate
We all, on this auspicious date;
But Jesus, reason for this tide,
Is oft forgotten far and wide.

So why not give *him* something, too?
A hymn? A pound! An hour? (or two!)
But is this right, when what I see:
The gift he really wants . . . is *me*.

Frank L Appleyard

OPEN IMMEDIATELY - GIFT ENCLOSED

Thank God for what the angels sang
Two thousand years ago -
A song that round the heavens rang
And on the Earth below -

About a gift to save mankind
From sin for evermore,
Wrapped up by God and pers'n'ly signed,
Delivered to our door.

No junk mail this, no catalogue,
No bill, but real free gift;
Enough to set your eyes agog
And give your heart a lift.

There is no closing date to beat,
Condition to be met,
Small print that will your eyes defeat -
Just payment of sin's debt.

So write your thank you letter quick
And send it back above;
It's postage paid, no stamp to stick.
Then live in heav'nly love.

David Varley

TWO HEARTS
(Abridged)

(I often think the Christmas scene . . . all snowy white and pure
Where a mother holds within her arms . . . her son to keep him warm)

She'd wrap Him in some swaddling clothes . . . this little babe of hers
Her heart was filled with so much joy . . .
She thought her heart would burst
She looked into those clear eyes . . . a depthless newborn's blue
To touch away a soulful tear . . . as soft as morning's dew

His fierce little newborn grip . . . wrapped a finger of her hand
And wrought a smile unto His lips . . . at her lullaby's soothing sound
Only once His eyes did wander . . . to smile on Joseph's face
Earth's and Heaven's hearts just then . . . together keeping pace?

His head slept to her bosom . . . as sleep fell to His eyes
While she His gentle forehead kissed . . . as in His sleep He sighed
Then a little baby shudder . . . perhaps it was the cold?
She hugged Him ever closer now . . . to the warmness of her soul

Soon shepherds and the herdsmen . . . shyly stood within
As three men who had travelled far . . . came offering gifts for Him
All this she now remembered . . . as she held Him once again
His broken body in her arms . . . another gift of men?

Oh my Son, my beautiful Son . . . oh my babe she cried
His lifeless body in her arms . . . her heart with Him had died
She held Him there, she brought Him close . . . held like that baby tight
The light of the world, within her arms . . . had left her soul as night

Those baby's eyes now bloodied . . . punched both black and blue
Those gentle lips she once had kissed . . . she no longer knew
Purpled by the brush of death . . . his hair all matted down
Dried sweat and bloodied scabs of skin . . . wrought by a thorny crown

She searched a face once beautiful . . . all but smashed and torn
For the face only a mother knows . . . on the day her Son is born
The second time His eyes left hers . . . dead in death just then
Earth's and Heaven's hearts awry . . . now wrenched apart by men

I often think the Christmas scene . . . and all there is to come
As once again within her arms . . . a mother holds her son?

M J Banasko

TWELFTH NIGHT

On the last day of Christmas
    as greedy as can be,
    my brother ate:

one lollipop,
        at the corner shop;

two sticky licks,
        as big as bricks;

three miners' hats,
        four cricket bats;

five bowls of custard,
        six jars of mustard;

seven icicles,
        eight bicycles;

nine apple tarts,
        ten water carts;

eleven chocolate bars,
        twelve motor cars;

then was sick over Grandma's new settee!

Alex Anderson

DISCARDED TREE

The sixth is here, we take the cards
And Christmas baubles down, restore
The room to routine's normal state.
On way to work I pass a tree
By wheelie bin. It's still adorned
For festive time, with pendant cans
That once were filled with beer. It seems,
For some, for Bacchus, not for Christ,
Is feast we've just indulged. Perhaps,
If truth be known, it's church that stole
A pagan binge to mark its birth.
This thought transforms initial shock
To sense of mirth. Besides, at feast
To mark a wedding, Christ once turned
Those jars of water into wine
Beyond compare. Despite the claims
Of those who think most fun is sin,
I'm sure that Jesus earned the jibe
That judged him only fit to drink
With those beneath contempt. With them
He found a lack of all pretence.
It's those who thought themselves above
The common herd he found absurd.
Perhaps those cans on tree are right
Conjunction praising life to full.

Henry Disney

CHRISTMAS MESSAGE

Our carols ring out very sweet
Along the lamp-lit frosty street
Singing of love and joy and cheer
For Christmas time is surely here.
We sing about our Saviour's birth
Of joy in Heaven and peace on Earth
When wise men came from lands afar
Led by a wondrous brilliant star.
Oh let us follow where it led
To Bethlehem's lowly cattle shed,
Where Mother Mary meek and mild,
Cradled in hay her little child.
In friendship let us give our hands
To people strange from far off lands,
And spread the message filled with love
God gave to man from Heaven above.

Margaret B Baguley

CHRISTMAS

The Christmas tree stands in the village square
Its myriad fairy lights attempting to display
The colourful delights the season brings
And, around its base, a group of choirboys sings
With such sweet sounds the shoppers gaze in awe
Captivated by both sight and sound.
Touched by the innocence of youth
Honoured by the giving of their time
Against the sharp, bright background
Of a manufactured snow
Angelic looking in the tree light's glow.

For just a while they listen,
Intently nonetheless
For just a while a bond prevails
A feeling of togetherness, of fellowship, of harmony,
A sense of peace, an easing of the weariness
An uplifting of the spirit
They move on, feeling more positive
To do chores, now more meaningful,
Thinking how well off they are
Thinking of those less fortunate
Remembering some whose Christmas can never be the same
A hurried, silent prayer of sympathy, of gratitude,
A deep sigh of contentment,
The Christmas spirit is reborn.

D J Totten

BUILD UP

Busy getting shopping before the Christmas rush,
Got my lists, all four of them I really need to rush,
First stop is the food and drink, the presents follow next,
Two lists gone, two to go, already feeling vexed.

I started out at half past eight now it's half past two,
All shopping done, no lists left, yet still there's lots to do,
The presents all assembled, the last bag's through the door,
All stacked upon the dining chairs and spilling to the floor.

The time is moving swiftly the children will be there,
Now to hide them all away, it's that special time of year,
The shed now out of limits, my wardrobe and the den,
Until I get them sorted out, and all wrapped up for them?

I'm totally exhausted it happens every year,
I wish I had a magic wand then Christmas would appear,
But I must get the tea on; find space for all the rest,
The drink's now in the garage locked in an old tin chest.

I've rearranged the cupboards, they're full up to the top,
We've got enough to see us through for weeks I needn't shop,
I do the same thing every year, I think it's for the best,
Just in time, here come the kids; bang goes my minute's rest.

K Townsley

CHRISTMAS

In the glowing embers of a Yuletide fire
We see faces of people we once knew,
Images of long departed loved ones
And for them we shed a tear or two.

But Christmas is not a time of sadness
With joy let your hearts abound;
Share your unbridled love this festive season
With the people all around.

Weep not for the dear departed
Think only of their achievements and be proud
And in the fire's glowing embers see them
As angels dancing on a cloud.

Gwen Liddy

CHRISTMAS CORRECTED

We three Kings of Orient are
Not allowed to travel afar
Those Herald Angels do not sing
We should not go a-carolling.

Our old idea of Xmas wrecked
By the politically correct
So Away in that far Manger
Could be a subject of great danger?

We'll have no Royal David's City
Nor first Noel . . . more's the pity
Oh Little Town of Bethlehem
Is not acceptable to them.

Singing Mary's Sweet Boy Child
Will be a custom quite reviled
Whilst 'Come All Ye Faithful'
Has been deemed distasteful.

If Good King Wenceslas now looked out
He would find killjoys about
And as for Silent Holy Night
It's now not calm, nor is it bright.

Why let these spoilsport derivations
Ban the ways of generations?
Political blackmail leave to those dutiful
While we sing All Things Bright and Beautiful!

Sarah Blackmore

ON MY OWN...

It's Christmas and I'm crying,
Don't know if I can cope,
Another Christmas without someone
It brings a lump to my throat.
I go and stay with family,
But they don't understand,
They think you can't be lonely
With people all around
I go through all the motions,
Smile with all the rest,
Open all the presents,
And try to do my best,
But I'm glad when it's over,
And I can go back home,
Because I'm not so lonely,
When I am on my own.

Margaret Berry

THANK GOD FOR CHRISTMAS

Let us remember on the 25th of December
When we are celebrating with friends and family.
That all the fun, and presents given
Would mean nothing if God in His heaven
Had not so loved the world that He gave us His only begotten Son

The most precious baby was born in a stable bare
The shepherds sent by angels came to stare.
All around the ox and ass were feeding there
And the wise men came later with gifts to share.

So do not forget to give a thought and thankful prayer
As you gather to enjoy the celebrating;
Remember, too, all those not as fortunate as you.
For that baby born on that first Christmas Day
Came to teach us all how to love and care - everyone.

Joan Earle Broad

PLEASE - DON'T SPOIL CHRISTMAS

The meaning of Christmas will not be lost,
Whilst our school teachers still make the effort
To make time, in school time, for our children
To put on plays of the birth.

Of Jesus the Saviour, from the Bible's old tale,
That all Christian folk read, and employ
The teachings therein, how to lead a good life,
Be honest and caring, live in peace on our beautiful Earth.

With the varied faiths and cultures, that our country's welcomed in,
Our new neighbours must respect our way of life,
The powers that govern this country of ours
Must not give in, to pressure to stop re-enacting this birth.

This pleasure all children enjoy, being part of the group
Must outweigh the prejudiced and fanatical ways,
Of other religions from all over the world,
Introducing comradeship to give little lives worth.

When all is said and done viewed through different eyes,
Whatever your faith, the same brief underlies
That our world was created by some major force,
By whatever name's given to its birth.

I hope no one deprives schools here in England the chance
To put on this annual display
The children so cute dressed in robes, crowns and wings,
And as lambs, joining together, in a stable, to witness a birth.

Sheila Bates

WINTER'S OPERETTA

Sounds of the valley come drifting through the night
Wild creatures hunting in starlight and moon's glow,
Through the trees see farmhouse window twinkling bright
It is winter, look at shadows darting o'er the snow.

Countryside in winter is a time of crystal wonderland
Footprints in the snow tell of who goes where, no disguise,
Frosty ferns hang from the hedges made by icy wind, are fanned
Round the barns and through the treetops Jack Frost cries.

The moonlight shines down on this stage where life's story is played,
A fox and rabbit, a mouse and owl round farm do act their part
Across the stillness of the night footsteps in the snow crunched,
                                                             then stayed,
A rush of air, a soft flap of wings hunter of the barn on stage
                                                                    does start.

Stagehands did not this operetta scenario make, just nature's hand,
These actors did not lines have to learn, no audience to applaud a skill,
This operetta and its players are made and taught by God's fine hand.
To see these actors from my window perform is pleasure
                                                                 that does thrill.

John Clarke

CHRISTMAS

Look around you and you may see
The fairy perched on the Xmas tree
Beautiful face and a golden dress
I wouldn't be happy with anything less
Spiced smelling candles around the fire
I wonder what our little hearts desire
Will Santa bring us what we want
Or will he end up stuck in the vault
Chestnuts, mistletoe, carols and hymns
Singing loudly of all our many sins
Before we know it it's gone again
Just as well to keep us all sane.

Gillian Ashe

FLANNEL ON A SNOWY AFTERNOON

From the solitude of a worn recliner,
he leapt in dreams across the grey outdoors,
one thickening curl encircled his pipe,
gnarled hands thumping the yellowed pages of a novel
he had no intention to read.
Another frosty log tossed into the dwindling hearth.
Another day, cold - best spent in bed,
or the next best thing;
crocheted across his knees,
a pair of tired leather toes peeking beneath
that hemmed drape strewn about the floor,
and flannel; soothing, soft and familiar,
as the cloistered remembrances
of one woman's touch about his waist,
Dresden tease, tender fingers upon his neck.

Some thirty years turned under grey,
riding the backward carousel of still images,
swirling, twirling, spattering along
as ticked half-frozen drops across the window.
Sliding, a streak, as though on a grand race
to their final collecting rest upon the sill.
If only the dragging hours knew their secrets well,
he wouldn't mind being alone,
in flannel, on this snowy afternoon.

Nick Zegarac

THE CHEERFUL POSTMAN

Skyline still holds the darkness, one hour left of night
Fine rain clouding his vision, through his torch's yellow light
Pedalling along in silence along the dampened half lit street
Passing the busy milkman, each other they daily greet.

Through curtains not quite drawn, the postman clearly sees
The glittering lights and baubles; that decorate the tinselled trees
At this sight he soon forgets, the chill of the winds that blow
When bending down to post those cards, through another box too low.

He's tries his best at all times, to some it seems not so
Perhaps his mind is elsewhere, as cards go to and fro
His mistakes he does amend when addresses are unclear
He corrects them with his knowledge, and tries again with cheer.

At Christmas time he knows you'll forgive him when you show
With delightful gifts and Christmas cards, on him you all bestow
Your kindness he'll not forget, and wants to be sincere
By staying as your cheerful postman; for at least another year.

Clive Goldsmith

CHORUS LINE

It was the Christmas panto
      at the Sunday school.
For weeks there'd been excitement,
      according to the rule.
Everyone must play a part
      to make it a good show.
Of course, there were the favourites
      just as you might well know.
Us girls, we were assembled
      in a line upon the stage.
Some were in their twelfth year
      but we didn't think of age.
We'd flutter in the spotlight
      a couple of minutes or so.
Then dance-step off into the wings -
      we knew the way to go.
Some boys upon the front row
      did point their fingers crude,
And shouted in derision
      some remarks quite rude.
For several nights the ordeal
      went on, until the time
They dropped the final curtain
      on my days in the chorus line.

Joyce Haigh

CHRISTMAS WISH

When love is born upon a Christmas Day
In a lowly manger filled with straw or hay
In two thousand years, we are still at war
The Prince of Peace, what did He die for,
We have not learnt the lesson yet
Forgive our brother less we forget
He is the same inside, like you and me
Though his skin, of a different
Colour may be, he's full of anger and pain
We live in hope, let peace remain,
Give our sister bread to feed her son
Let's start the work our Lord began.

Gatekeeper

CHRISTMAS: YULETIDE

Christmas, Yuletide, evergold and evergreen.
Full of merriment and mirth,
Set in the midst of the nativity scene,
Year after year, seemingly unchanging,
Which began some 2000 years ago,
With the Holy Child's birth.
As God, in human form, is born of Earth.

The British Christmas, set in a Victorian past,
The feasting and the festival,
Such midwinter merriment; long may it last.
Christmas trees and crackers,
Pantomime and party frocks.
Children anticipating Santa Claus,
As they ritually hang up their Christmas socks.
They eagerly count down the days.
Christmas Eve seems never ending,
As these little ones watch,
The slow movement of the fingers on the clock.

For all its commerciality; banality.
The stress that last minute Christmas shopping brings,
The day itself holds such magic,
A taste of Heaven,
With its offerings of hope, love and joy,
Which no other day can bring.
For on this special day,
Not only the cathedral choirs,
But our very hearts with elation sing.

Jonathan Pegg

THEN AND NOW

The Jews were waiting for a messiah
To free them from their woes,
But when You were born that winter night
They didn't want to know.

Your mother had to sleep with the stock
And lay You in a manger
Wild shepherds dancing in the street
Put Your life in danger.

Strangers coming from distant lands
Brought gifts of myrrh and gold
But from Your own You had to flee
When only a few days old.

Life hasn't changed much over the years
It's a world of steal and cheat
We welcome strangers from all the world
Our own can sleep in the street.

Joan M E Gray

A Tale Of Two Christmas'

People bustling,
in a crowded shop.
Tired and freezing,
at the bus stop.

Lights and tinsel,
make the house glow.
Heavy bags,
walking very slow.

Carol singers,
a distant church bell.
Ice on the steps,
the old lady fell.

Food, drink,
parties to go on.
Another night in,
no one to talk to.

Presents and gifts,
for everyone.
She thinks back,
remembers the fun.

Family and friends,
round the Christmas tree.
Cold and alone,
she has no one to see.

Gillian L Wise

CHRISTMAS CARD POEM - 2003

Scene on Christmas card I'm sending shows the clergy wish good day
To the folk who've been attending, as to home they wend their way.

Some stay standing there and talking with the vicar of St Peter's.
One young lady's swiftly walking, and has done a hundred metres.

Studying this long procession did suggest a race to me.
So I wrote a rhyme about it, which you are about to see:

Vicar starts the Christmas Stakes - the prize is Christmas Dinner.
Two at back are slow away, so they won't be the winner.

Then a couple, arm in arm - hardly in contention,
They won't cross the finish line before they draw their pension.

Talking mum holds tiny boy - leaning is his wish,
Like the 'leaning tower of weather' - dear old Michael Fish.

Family near Christmas tree would seem to be quick striders,
They could overtake the rest, so back them as outsiders.

Bessie Browncoat leads the field, but the bag she owns -
Might well prove a handicap, because it's filled with stones!

Three more people just behind might have filled the places,
But they are about to trip - up upon their laces!

One young lady stands and stares, dressed in coat of blue.
But she won't be winning cos she's stuck with Superglue!

'Who will win the Christmas Stakes', can I hear you say?
It will be the vicar, who's about to board his sleigh!

Alan Dudeney
(The Poet Laurie-ate - for breakfast)

CHRISTMAS STARS ON ASHDOWN FOREST

Ballyhoo the friendly badger, was making an announcement,
A meeting to be held, make some arrangements
Forest friends, meet in the enchanted glade,
Oscar Owl has news, a rehearsal is made.

Tomorrow is a special day, said Oscar,
The birth of a holy child, with our help will survive, and prosper.
Christmas Eve, is the day of preparation,
All contribute, let's make tomorrow a celebration.

Gerald, you and your family of glow-worms,
Generate extra light tonight, amongst the fern.
Sue and Sam Spider, please spin and weave your lacy webs,
Suspend them from the pine trees, to glitter, when daylight ebbs.

Man of Moon, will shine very brightly tonight,
His band of stars, send out rays, creating a spectacular sight.
The skies will be highlighted, by Solemn Star,
Who tonight will guide shepherds, travelling far.

Nicholas Nightingale, when the skies are aglow,
Please sing your best, and readily show,
Our forest friends, real beauty, of sound,
Notes to rise softly in slumber, until the baby is found.

Forest friends listened, watched, and wondered,
Darkness descended, excitement floundered, pondered,
A golden glow appeared, Man Moon, smiled his brightest smile,
Watching Gerald Glowworm's, glowing, there was no denial.

Sue and Sam's spider webs, were works of great beauty,
Glittering like jewels, Man Moon, twinkled,
Sue and Sam had done their duty.
Forest friends raised their heads, amazed at things they saw
The sky looked webbed in wonder, as if answering a call.

Nicholas Nightingale began to sing,
Solemn Star's rays glowed golden in Heaven.
His song filled the enchanted glade, echoing its way to Heaven,
The holy baby was born, inspiring forest friends,
With love on this special morn.

Oscar Owl knew his forest friends
Had learned something special this Christmas Eve,
The gift of love to cherish, and thankfully receive.

Lorna Tippett

The Message

Do we need the Christmas message,
Peace on Earth, goodwill to men?
Aren't we now sophisticated?
Haven't times moved on since then?

See the hungry babe who's crying,
Child of God, without a home;
See the refugee who's fleeing
Ask the victim of the bomb.

Go ask the bandit on the hillside,
Or the leaders in the city:
Ask the warlords wreaking havoc,
Killing, maiming without pity.

Go ask around the world's four corners,
Hear the weeping, only then:
Will we see the world so needing,
Peace on Earth, goodwill to men.

Rose Moss

A SNOWFLAKE FELL

A snowflake fell, the Christmas cake,
We have to bake, a fairy's spell,
The frosty shell, a frozen lake,
A snowflake fell.

All sing Noel, a tree we fell,
Now wide awake, the presents take,
The children make a magic dell.

The ringing bells, the snow we shake,
A pleasant smell, at lunch we dwell,
The wishing well do not forsake,
A snowflake fell.

David M Walford

Turkey

Cooling on a table on Christmas Day
I wonder: does it take an inquisition
to examine what the snugly-smug are
really feasting on amongst the stuffing
and the wishbones? They gather greedily
and gorge on giblet soup, as they begin
to doze in their accumulated fat.

Yesterday, the old heathens had a steak
or two for their beliefs: a spit of disdain
at the imposition cast against them.
Then toasting themselves, the bleating converts
marinated in lamb's wool, like vats of
swaggering surplices, swigging, as more
cracks of broken necks fell from the gibbets.

Today, baptised poults, born in innocence,
are trussed and basted and then warmed in the glow
of pre-packaged piety. The converts
lick their fingers in dribbling delight. Then
hold their parson's nose against the stench of
burning flesh from the glue factory down the
hungry rag-and-bone man's wintry road.

Amongst disbelief and dismemberment
I wonder: how is it possible to carve
your way through so many layers of dry,
processed gobbledegook without getting
near the bone? This might be my last supper,
but at least my broken, cold remains won't
flap and flop to anymore graceless games.

Ashley Smith

IT'S CHRISTMAS

Choirs will sing, bells will chime
Because it's a joyous Christmas time.
Children excited, and run about
'Santa's coming' they gleefully shout.
The festive cheer is everywhere
And shops are filled with Christmas fayre.
Houses light up the dismal dark night
The children gaze at the wondrous sight.

But Christmas is more than the glitz and fun
It is the birthday of God's only son.
When we remember that night long ago
In the dark sky a bright star did glow.
Shining over the stable where Mary gave birth
The son of God came to our Earth.
Shepherds and kings brought gifts to say
This shows our love, like we do today.

So let's not forget amidst all the fun
It all began with God's only son.

Lynne Walden

THOUGHTS AFTER CHRISTMAS

We went to the village this morning at nine,
And everyone's dustbin was out, just like mine.
And black bags of rubbish . . . too many to count
For something not needed, seemed such an amount.

I looked at the rubbish, and thought 'what's it worth
To celebrate Christmas, when Mary gave birth?'
I know that it happened a long time ago,
Before all the cards showing glitter and snow.

But now it seems Christmas has got out of hand
When I think of the money we spend in this land.
Not *just* on the children - the ones not in need
But think of the people that money could feed.

I'm clearing the tree out, the tinsel and chains.
But nuts, fruit and chocolate and the cake still remains.
Lying around, to be picked at our leisure,
We've eaten so much, it's past giving us pleasure.

We had a good Christmas, the best one for years,
With plenty of laughs, and some funny ideas.
And now it's all over the room's looking bare . . .
. . . I wonder if Mary would think it is fair

That while millions stuff themselves for a whole week
Millions more people less luxury seek.
We're all very lucky to live where we are.
We might have been born to just follow that star.

Jean Heath

FESTIVE FOLLY FROM A SILLY WALLY

Merry Christmas to you
For all the things that you do
May your wishes come true
Merry Christmas to you

Roast a turkey; ice a cake
Buy a pudding; you can bake
Pull a cracker; silly joke
Stupid hat; cigar to smoke

Cocktail sausage; cranberry sauce
Double video of Inspector Morse
Loads of cards; tinsel and a tree
Stuff a turkey and think of me!

Paul Foreman

CHRISTMAS EVE

The sky is splashed with wonder,
So clear with shining stars,
But peace is rent asunder
With noise from crowded bars.
Yet angel hosts are singing
If only we would hear
The news that they are bringing,
Their song of joy and cheer.
The stores, their pockets lining,
Distract us from the sound,
Whilst fairy lights are shining
Their glory all around.
Pause for a moment's stillness
To hear the angel song,
A halt to all the shrillness
From the pleasure-seeking throng.
Turn with expectant wonder
On this momentous eve,
And take some time to ponder
If you really can believe,
The angels with their tidings
Of an infant Saviour's birth,
They sing out Heaven's confiding
Of lasting peace on earth.
The news that God is coming
To dwell with splendour shorn,
A human form becoming
As the Christ-child is born.

J H Scrafton

A Christmas Stocking

A Christmas stocking?
Don't be so shocking!
It won't hold PlayStations
Computers or nations
Shopping with haste
For designer goods taste.
A Christmas stocking?
Don't be shocking!
It won't hold skateboards
Bikes for mountains, or camcorders.
Christmas stocking?
Yesterday's shopping
Was an apple, a pear,
A penny and there
Might have been sweets,
A book; but these treats
Were such a surprise -
But the real Christmas lies
In family and friends;
But *one family* sends
A message of peace
From a stable to reach
A world that's still seeking
The true Christmas meaning
By finding the way
To the love that one day
May fill all the earth -
Not just a stocking! The birth
Of God's Son for all,
No Santa Claus call
Can bring gifts so rare
For the whole world to share
As love, joy and peace topping
One great *Christmas stocking!*

Marion Skelton

A Time To Remember

The year is slowly slipping away,
The cold, bleak days are here to stay.
A flurry of snow, or driving rain,
Oh when will summer come again?

'What about Christmas?' I hear you say,
'It's only a couple of days away.
Think of the shopping still to be done,
I'm sure that will be a lot of fun.'

The trees are all arrayed with lights,
To help us brighten dreary nights.
The carol singers take their leave,
Reminding us it's Christmas Eve.

The children are tucked up in bed,
Remembering what Mother said.
That, 'Santa Claus will not appear,
Unless you are asleep, my dear.'

When they awake on Christmas morn,
The day that Jesus Christ was born.
They'll find beneath the Christmas tree,
Presents wrapped up for you and me.

It is a time of sheer delight,
For after waiting through the night,
The wrapping paper is quickly torn,
And all is revealed on Christmas morn.

But let us remember, this time of year,
Which brings us happiness, joy and cheer,
There is something we should go on believing,
It's a time for giving as well as receiving.

Keith C L Ball

THE TREE

Standing so proud adorned in its glory
The seasonal green giant takes centre stage
Creatively decorated with tinsel and baubles
Soft twinkling lights sparkle here and there
The fairy on top so proud she does stand
Does she really grant every wish that is made?
A mountain of gifts surround the base
Providing a garland of intrigue and delight
Carefully wrapped presents of all shapes and sizes
Each hopefully fulfilling a wish
Happiness, excitement and goodwill wishes
Making such a joyous Christmas time.

Anne Sackey

CHRISTMAS

Carol singing of Christmas cheer
Hark the herald angels singing here
Rudolph the red nosed reindeer
In the bleak midwinter saw 3 ships sailing bright
Santa coming to town on this silent night
Twelve days of Christmas and the three kings
Merry Christmas wishing all merry gentlemen
Ave Maria singing away in a manger
Saviour is born surrounded by angels.

P Brewer

CHRIST'S DAY - OR OURS?

Have we all forgotten,
Is it so hard to remember?
The reason why we celebrate
The 25th day of December.

It's the birthday of our Saviour,
And of course we're filled with joy.
But the reason should be the nativity
Not food and drink and toys.

It's a time for children to be happy
And for Santa Claus to bring his sack.
But not for spending what we can't afford
Then wondering how we'll pay it back.

At this time we should aim for peace,
And for doing what we can
To create the kind of world our Lord
Would have imagined in his plan.

But we know it will not be like that,
There will be family rows and fighting.
People drinking far too much
And doing other things - more frightening.

If only we could understand
Each others point of view.
Our aim should be for a world of peace
And a better future for me and you.

That would be a birthday gift
In which we all could have a say.
To remind us of the reason
Why we celebrate Christmas Day.

Gillian Edge

A Sense Of Christmas

Sparkling lights and stars and tinsel
Baubles hanging from the tree
Candles, cards, decorations and presents
Signs of Christmas for all to see

Carol singers, Christmas music
Sleigh bells tell us Santa's near
Crackers banging, church bells ringing
Signs of Christmas for all to hear

Christmas pudding, turkey, stuffing
Potatoes, parsnips, sprouts as well
Fir trees, mulled wine, scented candles
Signs of Christmas for all to smell

But 'mid all the celebrations
Take a moment to think and see
Without the baby in the manger
There would be no Christmas for you and me.

Claire Miller

A Fireside Story

Somewhere, a bell tolled midnight
Cold moonlight, saw children's tears
Cuddled up on a window seat of the bower
The Queen of night looked coldly on.

The shadowy reindeer, dipped heads
To the wide-eyed family group.
Speechless in the curtain folds.
Santa Claus himself, faded into the room

In utter silence, gifts from a great sack
Graced each bed, none for them it seemed
Little one smiled, ice melted on Santa's beard
Big smile, and was gone.

No word was spoken, sleep closed wet eyes
Morning came, white bearded man waited
''Tis Santa,' whispered a small voice
Wide eyes soon looked at snowy scenes

The big car glided down the lane
A smiling face, light streamed the path
Burning logs, chased the shadows
Garlands fluttered, a tree twinkled

Big sister said, 'They want us to stay'
And be our mum and dad
Little one said, 'Now I believe'
Dreams, can sometimes come truc.

H Cotterill

CHRISTMAS

Away in a manger a baby was born
That Christmas night, long, long ago.
The shepherds and wise men fell down on their knees
As the star shed its heavenly glow.
He came to bring peace to a world torn by strife
To bring love to a world ruled by hate
And he knew for that love he must die on the cross
Or the world would succumb to its fate.
It's 2000 years later, and still we don't see
Babies dying for lack of our care.
Their bellies distended, their mothers in tears.
We still haven't learned how to share.
In a land filled with plenty, there are those with no home.
No possessions, no money, no pride.
While the elderly cower behind bolted doors
Too frightened to venture outside.
We look to the heavens, but instead of the star
We see planes filled with weapons of war.
And the millions we spend on destruction and death
Could bring succour and hope to the poor.
And we still sing of peace and goodwill to all men.
Pray the lion will lay down with the lamb.
It's two thousand years on, we still worship the child
And drive nails through the hands of the man.

Ann Wood

CHRISTMAS STAR

Twinkle, twinkle, special star,
In the sky, up high, so far;
Like a carbonaceous gem
Beaming down on Jesse's stem.
Star of David, shining bright,
Hovering o'er the sacred site,
Guiding wise men along the way
To the King of Kings on a bed of hay.
Twinkle, twinkle, special star,
In the sky, up high, so far.

Kathy Rawstron

UNTITLED

Christmas time
the time of year
for giving and sharing
for laughter and tears

Families come together
and rejoice as one
lots of toys, lots of games
best of all, lots of fun

Children waiting anxiously
with faces all aglow
waiting for Santa
and hopefully snow.

Christmas Day dawns
and with it brings
lots of surprises
and special things.

The day soon ends
with happy children fast asleep
dreaming sweet dreams
forming memories they will keep.

Mary Patton

SANTA'S COMING

Santa is on his way
He'll ride across the sky
And pass a full moon by
With toys aboard his sleigh

Reindeer are set to go
They'll be pulling steady
For their load is heavy
Every home they know

Landing on the rooftops
Silently at each house
As quiet as a mouse
Leaving gifts at all stops

Children both large and small
Providing they've been good
All year long as they should
Can expect Santa's call

Names are all written down
Ev'ryone will be thrilled
Waking to dreams fulfilled
Proof Santa's been in town

Hark for reindeer running
Jingle bells soft and low
Or sounds of ho ho ho
That means Santa's coming.

Ladee Basset

CHRISTMAS - ENJOY OR ENDURE?

Enjoy the celebrations that get bigger every year
Endure the family quarrels - bound to reappear

Enjoy the office parties and dancing till you drop
Endure the greedy shoppers never knowing when to stop

Enjoy the youthful choristers singing songs that rhyme
Endure the saddened faces - the victims of a crime

Enjoy the expectations of the children that you meet
Endure the degradations of the homeless on the street

Enjoy the roasted turkey and the pudding and the wine
Endure the starving millions waiting patiently in line

Enjoy the whole world over who ring the Yuletide bell
Endure the heroin addict and his drug-inducing hell

Enjoy the decorations and the sparkling festive lights
Endure the wars on innocents and their piteous dying rites

Enjoy the day of Christmas and traditions of the past
But endure what comes tomorrow and the shadow it may cast.

Bernadette Ince

EARLY DECEMBER

Early December sees snow before the first day of winter
And on this day all is peaceful.

The solidarity reminds my mind there is truly peace so hard to find.
The naked spruce stands on my living room floor,
Exuding the fresh fragrance of winter green known years before.

White lights now glow around this tree of spruce.
And as the white snow falls, near is the season for peace and truth.

So, peace on Earth and gifts abundant;
The rush to buy seems meaningless and redundant.
Goodwill toward men, may your Christmas be pleasant;
The season brings meaning with just the right present.
Good tidings to you with your snifter of brandy;
A relaxed mind from bills soon due will come in handy.

I sip hot chocolate by the tree as white as the snow.
And breathe the aroma from the cinnamon candle's glow.
I think of Mary and Joseph and the divine birth of our saviour.
Is Christmas lost in the storm of our commercial behaviour?

Early December sees snow before the first day of winter
                                         and all is peaceful.
Where do all of my Christmas wishes begin?
With winter green spruce, hot chocolate, nutmeg and cinnamon,
Peace on Earth and goodwill toward men.

Kathy Flanary Nelson

TOMATO SAUCE

Spare a thought this Christmas
For all those desperate people,
Who will be alone or lonely
Those without family or friends,
To spend time with
Without Christmas warmth to receive or give.

While we sing Christmas carols,
Feel the spirit and cheer.
Pull crackers, read their mundane jokes aloud,
Wear silly hats, drink a little too much punch.
The lonely may raise a glass to the Queen's speech,
Then for their bangers and mash the tomato sauce reach.

For one man's Christmas cheer and joy,
Is probably another lonely's man's pretence that it matters not,
He won't allow himself a Christmas feeling,
As his Christmas Day passes with him trying to avoid the very word,
He sits, telling himself that it's all overrated, over the top!
While in the background, next door's celebrations echo non-stop.

It must be terrible to be lonely at Christmas,
Here in this land of milk and honey.
Bombarded by Christmas exploitation,
Where Christmas is commercialised for gain
And the true message of Christmas is somewhat obscure.
If ever I was forced to a solitary Christmas, I *couldn't*
Pretend that it just doesn't occur.

One solitary Christmas would be my last,
I'd book into a hotel or take myself off.
Somewhere people were plentiful and happy,
Keen to record another Christmas passing,
Keen to embrace Christmas warts and all.
Never to let their loneliness instead of Christmas cards
Hang from their wall.

P J Littlefield

THE ALTERNATIVE CHRISTMAS

My head's spinning round like a helter-skelter,
as I down a glass of Alka-Seltzer.
Too many mince pies, sherry and gin,
I've over indulged - now I'm sufferin'!
It's Christmas Day, and sheer mayhem
and it's only just turned 8am!
Turkey to stuff, cat's pulled tree onto floor
our guests have arrived, as my head throbs some more!
It's Auntie and Uncle with an armful of toys -
with two 'pinstriped' ties for my twin 6 year old boys!
And the look said it all from my 18 years old daughter
as she unwrapped the 'Barbie', auntie had bought her!
But we thanked them profusely, and said they were fine,
made polite conversation and sat down to dine.
Ten of us all including two cats
looked forward to lunch and wore paper hats.
Wine was now flowing, but one thing I've learnt -
don't have too many glasses, else lunch may be burnt!
As I entered the kitchen, I saw what awaited -
a shrivelled up turkey, and the veg all cremated!
The carrots and sprouts had both boiled dry
so I got out a pan and started to fry.
I rescued some cabbage, few 'taters, a leek
our Christmas lunch now would be 'bubble & squeak'!
Surprisingly so, lunch went like a dream -
though no one would try Christmas pudding and cream!
But we washed it all down with a nice glass of Hock
just in time for 'The Queen's Speech' at now 3 o'clock
with a glass of champagne we toasted the Queen
but Uncle proved to be not so keen
feet up on the sofa, one sock on - snoring
he's not patriotic, and finds royalty boring.

Still - he's full to the brim - my uncle Fred
'Best Christmas lunch ever!' is what Uncle said.
It's been an alternative Christmas, but one of good cheer
though it's your house next Christmas - have a happy new year!

Alison Jane Lambert

The Census In Bethlehem*

About faith and suffering
the Old Masters were never wrong.
Oh, a cold coming they had of it, it's true,
through cruel, untypical, midwinter, Flemish snow,
past the illegal settlements, avoiding
the Roman and Israeli checkpoints,
dodging the Semtex and the sniper's bullets.

The faith is in the detail,
and the detail's supranational, of all time.
Skaters in codpieces ignore the bureaucrats
studying lists, exacting tithes, demanding tribute.
Tree stumps suggest that fuel's in short supply.
Three scraggy pullets peck hard snow,
searching for nourishment.

Infants with sticks spin tops, guide basket-sledges
over ice. Men trudge, like thieves, in groups of three.
A makeshift abattoir. In solstice celebration, armed
with a knife, a peasant butcher flays a pig for Yule,
finding halal and kosher equally double-Dutch.
A barrel's broached. The beer of life is tapped.
A donkey bears a carpenter's pregnant wife.

Two thousand years ago, anachronisms did not
signify. Codpieces and stepped gables are not alien.
Bethlehem's Walloon, a mediaeval town.
A weak sun in the northern sky hangs low.
The ruined castle, decaying and decrepit,
sets off a building site where work's in progress.
Above a wattle hut, the cross stands etched,

a Christmas wreath rebukes the bureaucrats
and, on the hill, the church stands, open-doored.

** The reference is to Brueghel's painting in the
Musées Royaux des Beaux-Arts, Brussels.*

Norman Bissett

CHRISTMAS

Christmas is upon us,
The time is getting near
When Jesus came from Heaven
To be with us all here.

He is the Son of God,
The angels all declare,
In a stable He was born
With Mary and Joseph to care.

The shepherds came to see Him,
Their sheep and lambs they brought;
A symbol to remind us
Of a lesson to be taught.

A shining star brought wise men,
From the east they were led,
With gifts of gold, frankincense and myrrh
To lay down by His bed

And so among the shopping
And the gifts that we have bought,
Can we just stop and listen
And spare a special thought
Of when our Lord came down from Heaven
On that blessèd Christmas Day?

Christine

ANCHOR BOOKS
SUBMISSIONS INVITED
SOMETHING FOR EVERYONE

ANCHOR BOOKS GEN - Any subject, light-hearted clean fun, nothing unprintable please.

THE OPPOSITE SEX - Have your say on the opposite gender. Do they drive you mad or can we co-exist in harmony?

THE NATURAL WORLD - Are we destroying the world around us? What should we do to preserve the beauty and the future of our planet - you decide!

All poems no longer than 30 lines.
Always welcome! No fee!
Plus cash prizes to be won!

Mark your envelope (eg *The Natural World*)
And send to:
Anchor Books
Remus House, Coltsfoot Drive
Peterborough, PE2 9JX

**OVER £10,000 IN POETRY PRIZES
TO BE WON!**

Send an SAE for details on our latest competition!